Through ME JOURNAL
52 WEEKS DEVOTIONAL

THIS BOOK BELONGS TO :

COPYRIGHT © 2024 AJAY E SALAKO

All rights reserved. No part of this publication may be reproduced or transmitted in any form Or by any means, electronic or mechanical, including photocopy, recording, or any information Storage and retrieval system, without permission in writing from the publisher.

Introduction

Welcome to a transformative 52-week devotional journey that seeks to deepen your faith, encourage your heart, and inspire
a closer walk with God.
Each week offers an opportunity to meditate on Scripture, reflect on its truths, and draw strength from God's promises. Whether you're beginning your spiritual journey or seeking to strengthen your foundation, this devotional is designed to guide and uplift you week by week.
Together, we will explore themes of trust, hope, gratitude, and renewal,
All rooted in the timeless truths of God's Word.

Ajay E Salako

How This Book Works

This book is divided into 52 weeks, with each week thoughtfully structured into three main pages:

WEEKLY TITLE AND SCRIPTURE: Each week begins with a theme and a corresponding Scripture verse that sets the foundation for reflection and study.

DEVOTION: The second page offers a meaningful devotion that unpacks the week's Scripture, providing insights, encouragement, and practical applications for your daily life. These devotions are intentionally concise and impactful, helping you to connect deeply with God's Word.

PRAYER: The final page of each week includes a heartfelt prayer aligned with the theme, inviting you to bring your thoughts and reflections before God.

This simple yet profound structure ensures that you have a focused and consistent guide for your spiritual journey. Take your time with each week's content, allowing the Scriptures and prayers to resonate in your heart and inspire growth.

52 WEEKS
Devotional

BY AJAY E SALAKO

TODAY IS :   /   /

WHAT IS MY VIBE LIKE ?
COLOUR IN HOW VIBE YOU ARE FEELING

LOW VIBE   HIGH VIBE

WEEK 01
TRUST IN THE LORD

Proverbs 3:5-6
"Trust in the Lord with all your heart and lean not on your own understanding; in all your ways submit to him, and he will make your paths straight."

DEVOTIONAL

Life can be uncertain, and the weight of decisions often feels overwhelming. Yet, God calls us to trust Him completely. This trust requires surrender—letting go of our limited understanding and leaning on His infinite wisdom. When we submit to His guidance, we find clarity and peace.
God's plans are always greater than our own, and His timing is perfect. Take courage knowing He walks beside you. Trust opens the door to divine blessings and makes straight the path that seemed tangled. As you trust Him, rest assured that He is working all things together for your good.

PRAYER
Lord,

Teach me to trust You with my whole heart. Help me release my fears, doubts, and need for control. Guide my steps and make my path clear as I lean on Your wisdom. Strengthen my faith to follow You in all circumstances, knowing that Your plans for me are good.
Thank You for Your steadfast love and guidance. In Jesus' name, Amen.

REFLECTION

What are you must thankful for this week?

_____
_____
_____
_____
_____
_____
_____
_____
_____
_____
_____
_____
_____

TODAY IS :   /   /

WHAT IS MY VIBE LIKE ?
COLOUR IN HOW VIBE YOU ARE FEELING

LOW VIBE   HIGH VIBE

WEEK 02
GOD'S STRENGTH IN WEAKNESS

2 Corinthians 12:9
"My grace is sufficient for you, for my power is made perfect in weakness."

DEVOTIONAL

We often strive to appear strong, but God reminds us that His strength is revealed in our weakness. When we acknowledge our limitations, we create space for His power to work within us. His grace sustains us, even in our lowest moments. Rather than hiding your struggles, bring them to God. He delights in transforming weakness into strength. Remember, you don't have to carry life's burdens alone. Trust in His sufficiency and let His power renew you. Embrace your need for Him and watch how He works mightily in your life.

PRAYER
Father,

Thank You for Your sufficient grace.
In my moments of weakness, remind me that Your power is at work within me.
Help me to rely on You and not my own strength.
May I find rest in Your promises and peace in Your presence. Use my struggles to glorify You and draw me closer to Your heart.
In Jesus' name, Amen.

REFLECTION
What could have made this week better for you?

_____
_____
_____
_____
_____
_____
_____
_____
_____
_____
_____
_____
_____

TODAY IS :   /   /

WHAT IS MY VIBE LIKE ?
COLOUR IN HOW VIBE YOU ARE FEELING

LOW VIBE ▢ HIGH VIBE

WEEK 03
THE PEACE OF GOD

Philippians 4:7
"And the peace of God, which transcends all understanding, will guard your hearts and your minds in Christ Jesus."

DEVOTIONAL

Peace can feel elusive in a world filled with chaos. Yet, God offers us a peace that surpasses human comprehension. This peace is not tied to circumstances but rooted in His presence. When we bring our worries to Him in prayer, He replaces them with His calm assurance. Let God's peace guard your heart and mind like a fortress. Trust that He holds your future and is working for your good. No matter what you face, His peace is your anchor. Rest in the knowledge that He is in control and His love surrounds you.

PRAYER
Lord,

*Thank You for the gift of Your peace.
Help me to release my anxieties and trust in Your sovereign care. Guard my heart and mind against fear and doubt. Fill me with the assurance that You are always with me.
May Your peace reign in my life
and overflow to those around me.
In Jesus' name, Amen.*

REFLECTION

What you need to let go of so you can manifest better?

TODAY IS :   /   /

WHAT IS MY VIBE LIKE ?
COLOUR IN HOW VIBE YOU ARE FEELING

LOW VIBE 〔   〕 HIGH VIBE

WEEK 04
WALKING BY FAITH

2 Corinthians 5:7
"For we live by faith, not by sight."

DEVOTIONAL

Walking by faith requires stepping into the unknown, trusting that God is leading the way. It's not about seeing the whole path but about trusting the One who lights each step. Faith grows when we depend on God's promises, even when circumstances seem uncertain.

Let go of the need to control or understand everything. Trust that God's plan is unfolding perfectly, even if you can't see it yet. Take the next step in faith, knowing He is faithful to guide and provide. Faith transforms fear into courage and doubt into trust.

PRAYER
Heavenly Father,

Strengthen my faith as I walk through life's uncertainties. Teach me to trust You even when I can't see the way ahead. Remind me of Your promises and help me to stand firm on them. Guide my steps and fill my heart with confidence in Your plans.
Thank You for being my faithful Shepherd.
In Jesus' name, Amen.

REFLECTION
What is that thing you appreciate about yourself?

_____
_____
_____
_____
_____
_____
_____
_____
_____
_____
_____
_____
_____

TODAY IS :   /   /

WHAT IS MY VIBE LIKE ?
COLOUR IN HOW VIBE YOU ARE FEELING

LOW VIBE   HIGH VIBE

WEEK 05
GOD'S LOVE NEVER FAILS

Lamentations 3:22-23
"Because of the Lord's great love we are not consumed, for his compassions never fail. They are new every morning; great is your faithfulness."

DEVOTIONAL

God's love is steadfast and unfailing.
No matter how far you stray or how many times you fall,
His mercies are new every morning.
His faithfulness sustains us, even in our darkest moments.
You are deeply loved and cherished by the Creator
of the universe. Let this truth anchor you when doubts
arise. Rejoice in His constant presence and unchanging
love. As you start each day, remember that
His compassion is fresh and sufficient. Rest in the
assurance that nothing can separate you from His love.

PRAYER
Lord,

*Thank You for Your unfailing love and mercy. Help me to embrace Your compassion each day. Fill my heart with gratitude for Your faithfulness and draw me closer to You. May I live as a reflection of Your love, sharing it with those around me. Strengthen my trust in Your promises and remind me that I am never alone.
In Jesus' name, Amen.*

REFLECTION

What made today worth it ?

TODAY IS :   /   /

WHAT IS MY VIBE LIKE ?
COLOUR IN HOW VIBE YOU ARE FEELING

LOW VIBE □ HIGH VIBE

WEEK 06
REST IN GOD'S PRESENCE

Matthew 11:28
"Come to me, all you who are weary and burdened, and I will give you rest."

DEVOTIONAL

Life's demands often leave us feeling exhausted and overwhelmed. Yet, Jesus invites us to find rest in Him. His rest is not just physical but deeply spiritual, renewing our souls. When we surrender our burdens to Him, He replaces them with His peace. Resting in God means trusting Him with every aspect of our lives.
Take time to pause, breathe, and reconnect with His presence. Let Him refresh your spirit and fill you with His strength. Rest is not a luxury; it's a gift from a loving Father who cares for you.

PRAYER
Lord,

I bring my burdens and weariness to You. Teach me to rest in Your presence and rely on Your strength. Quiet my heart and renew my spirit as I trust in Your care.
Help me to let go of what weighs me down and embrace Your peace. Thank You for the gift of rest and the promise of renewal.
In Jesus' name, Amen.

REFLECTION
When was the last time you felt loved and appreciated?

TODAY IS :   /   /

WHAT IS MY VIBE LIKE ?
COLOUR IN HOW VIBE YOU ARE FEELING

LOW VIBE | | HIGH VIBE

WEEK 07

GOD'S FAITHFULNESS

Deuteronomy 7:9
*"Know therefore that the Lord your God is God;
He is the faithful God, keeping his covenant
of love to a thousand generations of those who love
Him and keep his commandments."*

DEVOTIONAL

God's faithfulness is unchanging and enduring.
He keeps His promises and never falters.
Even when life feels uncertain, you can trust that
He remains steadfast. Reflect on the countless ways
He has shown His faithfulness in your life.
His love and commitment extend through generations,
anchoring us in hope. Hold onto His Word, for it is a firm
foundation. No matter what challenges arise,
remember that He is faithful to lead, protect, and provide.
Rest in the assurance that His faithfulness will never fail.

PRAYER
Father,

*Thank You for Your unwavering faithfulness. Remind me of Your promises and help me to trust in Your Word. Strengthen my faith when doubts arise and guide me with Your steadfast love.
May my life reflect my gratitude for Your constant presence. Thank You for being the faithful God I can always rely on.
In Jesus' name, Amen.*

REFLECTION

Who loves and support you no matter what?

_____
_____
_____
_____
_____
_____
_____
_____
_____
_____
_____
_____
_____
_____
_____

TODAY IS :   /   /

WHAT IS MY VIBE LIKE ?
COLOUR IN HOW VIBE YOU ARE FEELING

LOW VIBE   HIGH VIBE

WEEK 08
BE STILL AND KNOW

Psalm 46:10
"Be still, and know that I am God;
I will be exalted among the nations,
I will be exalted in the earth."

DEVOTIONAL

In the busyness of life, it's easy to lose sight of God's presence. Yet, He calls us to be still and recognize His sovereignty. Being still doesn't mean inactivity; it means trusting God and resting in His control. In moments of quiet, we hear His voice more clearly. Let go of striving and allow Him to work in your life. Stillness is an act of faith, acknowledging that He is greater than your circumstances. Find peace in knowing that He is God and that His plans are perfect.

PRAYER
Lord,

*Teach me to be still and trust in You.
Quiet my anxious thoughts and remind me
of Your power and love. Help me to surrender
control and rest in Your presence.
Open my heart to hear Your voice and follow
Your guidance. Thank You for being
the God who is always near.
In Jesus' name, Amen.*

REFLECTION

Do you feel blessed and if yes count your blessings till you run out of space

_____
_____
_____
_____
_____
_____
_____
_____
_____
_____
_____
_____
_____
_____
_____

TODAY IS :   /   /

WHAT IS MY VIBE LIKE ?
COLOUR IN HOW VIBE YOU ARE FEELING

LOW VIBE   HIGH VIBE

WEEK 09

THE LIGHT OF THE WORLD

John 8:12
*"When Jesus spoke again to the people, He said,
'I am the light of the world. Whoever follows me will never
walk in darkness, but will have the light of life.'"*

DEVOTIONAL

Jesus is the light that dispels all darkness.
In Him, we find clarity, direction, and hope.
When the world feels dark and uncertain,
His light guides our path. Walking in His light means
living in His truth and love. Let His presence illuminate
your heart and dispel fear and doubt. As His followers,
we are also called to reflect His light to others.
Shine brightly, knowing that His light within you
can bring hope to those around you.
Embrace the light of life that only Jesus provides.

PRAYER
Jesus,

*Thank You for being the light in my life.
Help me to walk in Your truth and reflect
Your love to the world. Guide me through
the darkness and fill me with Your hope.
Use me to be a beacon of light for those in need.
Thank You for the promise of life and direction
through You.
In Your name, Amen.*

REFLECTION
Use your imagination and write down
the life you want for yourself

_____
_____
_____
_____
_____
_____
_____
_____
_____
_____
_____
_____
_____
_____

TODAY IS :   /   /

WHAT IS MY VIBE LIKE ?
COLOUR IN HOW VIBE YOU ARE FEELING

LOW VIBE   HIGH VIBE

WEEK 10
THE GOOD SHEPHERD

John 10:11
"I am the good shepherd. The good shepherd lays down his life for the sheep."

DEVOTIONAL

Jesus, the Good Shepherd, knows and cares for His sheep intimately. He leads, protects, and provides for us, even at the cost of His own life. In His care, we find safety and belonging. When we wander, He seeks us and brings us back to His fold. Trust in His guidance and rest in His love. He laid down His life to save us, demonstrating the depth of His commitment. Follow Him with confidence, knowing that He will never abandon you.
His love as the Good Shepherd is unending and personal.

PRAYER

Lord Jesus,

Thank You for being my Good Shepherd. Guide me with Your wisdom and protect me with Your love.
Help me to trust Your leadership and follow You faithfully. Thank You for laying down Your life for me and for always seeking me when I stray. May I rest in the assurance of Your care.
In Your name, Amen.

REFLECTION

How often do you take your Self care seriously?

TODAY IS :   /   /

WHAT IS MY VIBE LIKE ?
COLOUR IN HOW VIBE YOU ARE FEELING

LOW VIBE [   ] HIGH VIBE

WEEK 11
STRENGTH IN WEAKNESS

2 Corinthians 12:9
"But he said to me, 'My grace is sufficient for you, for my power is made perfect in weakness.' Therefore I will boast all the more gladly about my weaknesses, so that Christ's power may rest on me."

DEVOTIONAL

Our weaknesses can often feel like obstacles,
but God uses them to display His strength.
When we acknowledge our need for Him,
His grace becomes our source of power.
Instead of hiding our struggles, we can bring them before
God, trusting that He will work through them.
His grace is sufficient to sustain us in every season.
Allow His power to shine through your vulnerabilities,
and rest in the assurance that He is with you.
His strength is perfected when we rely fully on Him.

PRAYER
Lord,

Thank You for Your grace that sustains me. Teach me to embrace my weaknesses, knowing that Your power is made perfect in them. Help me to rely on You in every challenge and to trust in Your strength. May Your grace empower me to live boldly for You.
In Jesus' name, Amen.

REFLECTION
When was the last time you gave
to a stranger or someone in need?

_____
_____
_____
_____
_____
_____
_____
_____
_____
_____
_____
_____
_____
_____

TODAY IS :   /   /

WHAT IS MY VIBE LIKE ?
COLOUR IN HOW VIBE YOU ARE FEELING

LOW VIBE   HIGH VIBE

WEEK 12
THE FAITHFULNESS OF GOD

Lamentations 3:22-23
"Because of the Lord's great love we are not consumed, for his compassions never fail. They are new every morning; great is your faithfulness."

DEVOTIONAL

God's faithfulness is unchanging and constant. Every day, His mercies are new, and His love never fails. No matter what we face, we can rest in the assurance that He is faithful to His promises. Trust in His faithfulness, knowing that He will never leave you or forsake you.

PRAYER
Lord,

Thank You for Your unwavering faithfulness. I trust in Your promises and rely on Your love and compassion. Help me to remain faithful to You as You remain faithful to me.
Amen.

REFLECTION
When was the last time you prayed and felt like you got an instant answer?

TODAY IS :   /   /

WHAT IS MY VIBE LIKE ?
COLOUR IN HOW VIBE YOU ARE FEELING

LOW VIBE   HIGH VIBE

WEEK 13
LIVING WATER

John 4:14
"But whoever drinks the water I give them will never thirst. Indeed, the water I give them will become in them a spring of water welling up to eternal life."

DEVOTIONAL

Jesus offers living water that quenches the deepest
thirst of our souls. This living water is His Spirit,
bringing eternal life, peace, and satisfaction.
No worldly source can truly fulfill us like He can.
When we draw close to Him, He fills us with His presence,
and we become a source of life to others. Just as water
sustains physical life, His Spirit sustains our spiritual life.
Drink deeply from His well of grace
and find refreshment for your soul.

PRAYER
Lord,

Thank You for offering me the living water of Your Spirit. Quench my thirst for meaning and fulfillment with Your love.
Help me to seek You daily and be a source of encouragement to others. Fill me with Your presence, and let Your life flow through me.
In Jesus' name, Amen.

REFLECTION

What are the things you wished you can improve about yourself ?

_____
_____
_____
_____
_____
_____
_____
_____
_____
_____
_____
_____
_____

TODAY IS :   /   /

WHAT IS MY VIBE LIKE ?
COLOUR IN HOW VIBE YOU ARE FEELING

LOW VIBE │   │ HIGH VIBE

WEEK 14
A HEART OF GRATITUDE

1 Thessalonians 5:18
"Give thanks in all circumstances;
for this is God's will for you in Christ Jesus."

DEVOTIONAL

Gratitude transforms our hearts and minds,
drawing us closer to God. Even in difficult seasons, there's
always a reason to be thankful. Recognizing
His blessings shifts our focus from what we lack to what
He has provided. Gratitude strengthens our faith and helps
us see God's hand at work. Practice giving thanks daily,
not only for blessings but also for challenges that shape
you. A heart of gratitude leads to joy and deeper
trust in God's plan for your life.

PRAYER

Father,

*Thank You for Your countless blessings in my life.
Teach me to give thanks in all circumstances,
trusting in Your plan.
Open my eyes to see Your goodness even in trials.
Fill my heart with gratitude and joy as
I walk in Your will.
In Jesus' name, Amen.*

REFLECTION

What opportunity did you have this week?

_____
_____
_____
_____
_____
_____
_____
_____
_____
_____
_____
_____
_____
_____

TODAY IS :   /   /

WHAT IS MY VIBE LIKE ?
COLOUR IN HOW VIBE YOU ARE FEELING

LOW VIBE | | HIGH VIBE

WEEK 15
THE POWER OF FORGIVENESS

Matthew 6:14
"For if you forgive other people when they sin against you, your heavenly Father will also forgive you."

DEVOTIONAL

Forgiveness is both a gift we receive and a command we are called to obey. Letting go of hurt and resentment frees us from the weight of bitterness.

Jesus forgave us completely, and He empowers us to extend that same grace to others. Forgiveness doesn't mean excusing wrongdoing, but it does mean releasing the offender to God. As you forgive, you open your heart to healing and reconciliation.

Trust God to work through the process of forgiveness and bring peace to your relationships.

PRAYER

Lord,

*Thank You for forgiving me through Christ. Help me to forgive others as You have forgiven me. Release me from bitterness and fill my heart with Your grace. Teach me to trust in Your justice and to let go of offenses. Thank You for the freedom that comes through forgiveness.
In Jesus' name, Amen.*

REFLECTION

What do you appreciate about yourself everyday?

_____
_____
_____
_____
_____
_____
_____
_____
_____
_____
_____
_____

TODAY IS :   /   /

WHAT IS MY VIBE LIKE ?
COLOUR IN HOW VIBE YOU ARE FEELING

LOW VIBE │   │ HIGH VIBE

WEEK 16
GOD'S UNFAILING LOVE

Romans 8:39
"Neither height nor depth, nor anything else in all creation, will be able to separate us from the love of God that is in Christ Jesus our Lord."

DEVOTIONAL

God's love for us is unconditional and unchanging.
No matter where we go, what we do, or how we feel,
His love will never fail. It is a constant source of strength
and comfort. Even when we feel distant or unworthy,
God's love never wavers. In every season of life,
His love surrounds us, keeping us secure. We are cherished
beyond measure, and that love is always available to us.

PRAYER
Lord,

Thank You for Your unfailing love. Help me to feel the depth of Your affection every day, and remind me that nothing can separate me from You. When I feel lost, let Your love be my anchor. Amen.

REFLECTION
Write a short letter to your creator,
be transparent with him.

_____
_____
_____
_____
_____
_____
_____
_____
_____
_____
_____
_____

TODAY IS :   /   /

WHAT IS MY VIBE LIKE ?
COLOUR IN HOW VIBE YOU ARE FEELING

LOW VIBE ⸺⸺⸺⸺⸺⸺⸺⸺⸺⸺ HIGH VIBE

WEEK 17
THE GIFT OF GRACE

Ephesians 2:8-9
"For it is by grace you have been saved, through faith—and this is not from yourselves, it is the gift of God—not by works, so that no one can boast."

DEVOTIONAL

Grace is an undeserved gift from God. We cannot earn it, but we receive it through faith in Jesus Christ.
It is through grace that we are saved and made new. Remember, grace is not based on our actions or worthiness—it is purely God's gift of love and mercy.

PRAYER
Lord,

Thank You for the gift of grace. I am humbled by Your unmerited favor and salvation. Help me to live in a way that reflects Your grace to others. Amen.

REFLECTION

What have you learned from a difficult situation this week?

_____
_____
_____
_____
_____
_____
_____
_____
_____
_____
_____
_____

TODAY IS :   /   /

WHAT IS MY VIBE LIKE ?
COLOUR IN HOW VIBE YOU ARE FEELING

LOW VIBE │   │ HIGH VIBE

WEEK 18
ENDURANCE THROUGH TRIALS

James 1:2-4
*"Consider it pure joy, my brothers and sisters, whenever you face trials of many kinds, because you know that the testing of your faith produces perseverance.
Let perseverance finish its work so that you may be mature and complete, not lacking anything."*

DEVOTIONAL

Trials and challenges are a part of life,
but they are also an opportunity for growth.
As we face difficulties, God uses them to strengthen our
faith and build perseverance. Instead of being discouraged,
we can find joy in the process, knowing that through the
trials, God is shaping us into who He wants us to be.

PRAYER
Lord,

Help me to endure through trials with joy, knowing that You are using them to strengthen my faith. Give me perseverance and patience as I trust in Your perfect work in me.
Amen.

REFLECTION

What stopped you from working towards your goals this week?

TODAY IS :   /   /

WHAT IS MY VIBE LIKE ?
COLOUR IN HOW VIBE YOU ARE FEELING

LOW VIBE ⬜ HIGH VIBE

WEEK 19
WALKING BY FAITH

2 Corinthians 5:7
"For we live by faith, not by sight."

DEVOTIONAL

Faith is not always easy, especially when we can't see the path ahead. Yet, God calls us to trust Him, even in the uncertainty. Walking by faith means believing in His promises, even when the situation doesn't look promising. Trust that God is leading you and will provide exactly what you need. Let your faith be the foundation of your journey, knowing He is with you every step.

PRAYER
Lord,

Help me to walk by faith and not by sight. Strengthen my trust in You, especially when the way forward is unclear. I place my hope in Your guidance and provision.
Amen.

REFLECTION

Your favorite childhood dreams?

___
___
___
___
___
___
___
___
___
___
___
___

TODAY IS :   /   /

WHAT IS MY VIBE LIKE ?
COLOUR IN HOW VIBE YOU ARE FEELING

LOW VIBE　　　　　　　　　　　　　　　　　　　　HIGH VIBE

WEEK 20
GOD'S PROVISION

Philippians 4:19
"And my God will meet all your needs according to the riches of his glory in Christ Jesus."

DEVOTIONAL

God promises to provide for all our needs — emotionally, spiritually, and physically. His provision is abundant and perfectly timed. We may not always receive what we expect, but we can trust that God knows what is best for us. When we seek Him first, He takes care of us in ways we may not even realize. Trust in His provision and know that He will never leave you lacking.

PRAYER
Lord,

Thank You for Your abundant provision. I trust that You will meet all my needs according to Your glorious riches. Help me to rely on You fully, knowing You are my source of all good things.
Amen.

REFLECTION

Do you believe in yourself or you're struggling from self doubt?

TODAY IS :   /   /

WHAT IS MY VIBE LIKE ?
COLOUR IN HOW VIBE YOU ARE FEELING

LOW VIBE HIGH VIBE

WEEK 21

REST IN GOD'S PEACE

John 14:27

*"Peace I leave with you; my peace I give you.
I do not give to you as the world gives.
Do not let your hearts be troubled and do not be afraid."*

DEVOTIONAL

In a world filled with noise and chaos, God offers us a peace that surpasses understanding. His peace isn't based on circumstances but on His presence. When we invite Him into our hearts, He calms our anxieties and fills us with a deep, unshakable peace. Let go of worry and embrace His peace. Trust that He is in control, and His peace will guide you.

PRAYER
Lord,

*I invite Your peace into my heart.
Calm my anxious thoughts and help me to rest in
Your presence. Thank You for the peace that only
You can give. I trust that You are always with me.
Amen.*

REFLECTION
From the scale of 1-10 how much confidence
do you have in yourself and why?

TODAY IS :   /   /

WHAT IS MY VIBE LIKE ?
COLOUR IN HOW VIBE YOU ARE FEELING

LOW VIBE ▢ HIGH VIBE

WEEK 22
LIVING WITH PURPOSE

Jeremiah 29:11
"For I know the plans I have for you," declares the Lord, "plans to prosper you and not to harm you, plans to give you a hope and a future."

DEVOTIONAL

God has a unique and beautiful purpose for each of us. His plans are always good, even when we can't see the whole picture. Trust that God is leading you toward your destiny. Every step you take, whether big or small, is part of His greater plan. Live each day with intention, knowing that you are fulfilling His purpose for your life.

PRAYER
Lord,

Thank You for the purpose You've set for my life. Help me to trust in Your plan, even when it's not clear to me. Guide me in fulfilling the purpose You have designed for me.
Amen.

REFLECTION

Do you feel special ?

_____
_____
_____
_____
_____
_____
_____
_____
_____
_____
_____
_____

TODAY IS :   /   /

WHAT IS MY VIBE LIKE ?
COLOUR IN HOW VIBE YOU ARE FEELING

LOW VIBE   HIGH VIBE

WEEK 23
THE GIFT OF GRATITUDE

1 Thessalonians 5:18
*"Give thanks in all circumstances;
for this is God's will for you in Christ Jesus."*

DEVOTIONAL

Gratitude transforms our hearts and perspectives.
In every situation, there is something to be thankful
for — even in hardship. God is always working for our
good, and when we choose gratitude, we align our hearts
with His will. Cultivate a heart of thankfulness,
knowing that each moment is a gift.
Let gratitude be a reflection of God's goodness in your life.

PRAYER
Lord,

Thank You for all the blessings You've given me. Help me to be thankful in all circumstances, recognizing Your hand in every part of my life. May my heart overflow with gratitude for Your goodness.
Amen.

REFLECTION

What make you and high valued person?

___
___
___
___
___
___
___
___
___
___
___
___
___
___
___

TODAY IS :   /   /

WHAT IS MY VIBE LIKE ?
COLOUR IN HOW VIBE YOU ARE FEELING

LOW VIBE   HIGH VIBE

WEEK 24
LIVING IN FREEDOM

Galatians 5:1
"It is for freedom that Christ has set us free.
Stand firm, then, and do not let yourselves
be burdened again by a yoke of slavery."

DEVOTIONAL

Christ has set us free from the bondage of sin and shame. We are no longer slaves to fear, guilt, or worldly expectations. In His freedom, we can live fully and boldly, knowing that we are forgiven and loved. Stand firm in the freedom Christ has given you, and refuse to let anything hold you back from living in His grace.

PRAYER
Lord,

Thank You for the freedom You've given me in Christ. Help me to live boldly in that freedom, free from fear and shame.
Teach me to stand firm in Your truth and grace.
Amen.

REFLECTION

Do you love yourself and are you worthy of the love you expect from others?

TODAY IS :   /   /

WHAT IS MY VIBE LIKE ?
COLOUR IN HOW VIBE YOU ARE FEELING

LOW VIBE │   │ HIGH VIBE

WEEK 25
SEEKING GOD'S KINGDOM

Matthew 6:33
"But seek first his kingdom and his righteousness, and all these things will be given to you as well."

DEVOTIONAL

When we prioritize God's kingdom above all else,
everything else falls into place. Seeking His righteousness
means living according to His will, trusting Him to provide
for our needs. Let your focus be on God's work
and His ways, and He will take care of the rest.
In seeking Him first, we find fulfillment,
peace, and purpose.

PRAYER
Lord,

Help me to seek Your kingdom first. Guide me to live according to Your will and trust You for all I need. I want to honor You above all else, knowing You will provide for me.
Amen.

REFLECTION

What is your love language ?

TODAY IS :   /   /

WHAT IS MY VIBE LIKE ?
COLOUR IN HOW VIBE YOU ARE FEELING

LOW VIBE   HIGH VIBE

WEEK 26
THE POWER OF PRAYER

Philippians 4:6-7
"Do not be anxious about anything, but in every situation, by prayer and petition, with thanksgiving, present your requests to God. And the peace of God, which transcends all understanding, will guard your hearts and your minds in Christ Jesus."

DEVOTIONAL

Prayer is our direct communication with God.
Through prayer, we can bring our anxieties, worries,
and requests before Him. God promises that when we pray,
His peace will guard our hearts and minds.
Prayer is a powerful tool that brings us closer to God
and helps us experience His peace in every circumstance.

PRAYER
Lord,

Thank You for the gift of prayer. Help me to bring everything to You in prayer, trusting in Your peace and provision. Guard my heart and mind with Your peace that surpasses understanding. Amen.

REFLECTION

What your favourite time of the year and why ?

TODAY IS :   /   /

WHAT IS MY VIBE LIKE ?
COLOUR IN HOW VIBE YOU ARE FEELING

LOW VIBE ▭ HIGH VIBE

WEEK 27
OVERCOMING FEAR

Isaiah 41:10
"So do not fear, for I am with you; do not be dismayed, for I am your God. I will strengthen you and help you; I will uphold you with my righteous right hand."

DEVOTIONAL

Fear has no place in our lives when we trust in God. He promises to strengthen and help us, no matter what challenges we face. When fear rises, turn to God for courage, knowing He is always with you.
His presence is greater than any fear, and He will uphold you with His mighty hand. You are not alone.

PRAYER
Lord,

Thank You for Your presence that drives out fear. Help me to trust in Your strength and not be overwhelmed by anxiety. Let Your peace replace my fears and remind me of Your constant help. Amen.

REFLECTION

Something in your daily routing that brings you joy?

_____
_____
_____
_____
_____
_____
_____
_____
_____
_____

TODAY IS : / /

WHAT IS MY VIBE LIKE ?
COLOUR IN HOW VIBE YOU ARE FEELING

LOW VIBE ☐ HIGH VIBE

WEEK 28
GOD'S TIMING

Ecclesiastes 3:11
*"He has made everything beautiful in its time.
He has also set eternity in the human heart; yet no one
can fathom what God has done from beginning to end."*

DEVOTIONAL

God's timing is always perfect, even when it doesn't align with our own expectations. Trust that He is working behind the scenes, preparing the right moments for His plan to unfold. When we try to rush or force things, we miss out on His perfect timing.
Have faith that everything will happen at the right moment, and rest in the beauty of God's timing.

PRAYER
Lord,

*Help me to trust in Your perfect timing.
When I feel impatient or unsure, remind me that
You are always in control. I rest in Your timing,
knowing You are orchestrating everything
for my good.
Amen.*

REFLECTION

When was the last time you took yourself on a date?

TODO IS :   /   /

WHAT IS MY VIBE LIKE ?
COLOUR IN HOW VIBE YOU ARE FEELING

LOW VIBE　　　　　　　　　　　　　　　　　　HIGH VIBE

WEEK 29
LIVING WITH GRATITUDE

1 Thessalonians 5:16-18
"Rejoice always, pray continually,
give thanks in all circumstances;
for this is God's will for you in Christ Jesus."

DEVOTIONAL

Gratitude is a choice, and it is a powerful way to align our hearts with God's will. No matter what our circumstances may be, we are called to rejoice, pray, and give thanks. Gratitude shifts our focus from what we lack to what God has already done in our lives, bringing joy and peace.

PRAYER
Lord,

*Help me to live with a heart of gratitude.
In every situation, may I choose to rejoice and
give thanks for Your blessings. Teach me to focus
on Your goodness and faithfulness.
Amen.*

REFLECTION

What is the moment that made you fulfilled ?

_____
_____
_____
_____
_____
_____
_____
_____
_____
_____
_____

TODAY IS :   /   /

WHAT IS MY VIBE LIKE ?
COLOUR IN HOW VIBE YOU ARE FEELING

LOW VIBE   HIGH VIBE

WEEK 30
RESTORING HOPE

Romans 15:13
*"May the God of hope fill you with all joy
and peace as you trust in him, so that you may overflow
with hope by the power of the Holy Spirit."*

DEVOTIONAL

In times of despair, God is our source of hope.
He fills us with joy and peace, even when the world
around us feels uncertain. Hope is not based on
circumstances, but on God's faithfulness. As we trust Him,
His hope overflows in us, becoming a beacon for others.
Hold on to the hope that is found in Him, knowing
He is working all things for your good.

PRAYER
Lord,

Restore my hope. When I feel overwhelmed, remind me of Your faithfulness and the hope I have in You. Fill me with joy and peace as I trust in Your promises.
Let Your hope overflow in me.
Amen.

REFLECTION

How well do you know your family ?

_____
_____
_____
_____
_____
_____
_____
_____
_____
_____
_____
_____

TODAY IS :   /   /

WHAT IS MY VIBE LIKE ?
COLOUR IN HOW VIBE YOU ARE FEELING

LOW VIBE [   ] HIGH VIBE

WEEK 31
GOD'S PEACE IN THE STORM

John 14:27
"Peace I leave with you; my peace I give you.
I do not give to you as the world gives.
Do not let your hearts be troubled and do not be afraid."

DEVOTIONAL

God's peace is different from the peace the world offers.
It's a peace that calms our hearts and minds, no matter the
circumstances. When we face storms in life,
we can trust in the peace that only God provides.
Jesus promises to give us His peace to guard
us through every trial.

PRAYER
Lord,

*Thank You for the peace You give me.
In the midst of my storms, help me to rest
in Your peace and trust that You are in control.
Calm my heart and help me to experience
Your peace that transcends understanding.
Amen.*

REFLECTION

What talent do you have that you're proud of ?

TODAY IS :   /   /

WHAT IS MY VIBE LIKE ?
COLOUR IN HOW VIBE YOU ARE FEELING

LOW VIBE   HIGH VIBE

WEEK 32
GOD'S PROTECTION

Psalm 91:11
"For he will command his angels concerning you to guard you in all your ways;"

DEVOTIONAL

God promises to protect us with His divine presence. His angels watch over us, guarding us from harm and guiding us through danger. We are never alone in our struggles, as God's protection surrounds us.
Trust in His ability to keep you safe, both physically and spiritually. Rest in the assurance that
He is always watching over you.

PRAYER
Lord,

*Thank You for Your protection.
I trust that You are keeping me safe,
guiding me through life's challenges.
Surround me with Your angels
and guard me in all my ways.
Amen.*

REFLECTION

What makes you stand out ?

TODAY IS :   /   /

WHAT IS MY VIBE LIKE ?
COLOUR IN HOW VIBE YOU ARE FEELING

LOW VIBE   HIGH VIBE

WEEK 33
LIVING BY THE SPIRIT

Galatians 5:25
*"Since we live by the Spirit,
let us keep in step with the Spirit."*

DEVOTIONAL

The Holy Spirit is our guide and comforter,
empowering us to live according to God's will.
To live by the Spirit means to align our hearts and actions
with His leading. This requires listening carefully and
responding in obedience. The more we surrender
to His guidance, the more we experience the fullness
of God's purpose for our lives.

PRAYER
Holy Spirit,

Lead me in every step I take.
Help me to follow Your guidance
and live in obedience to Your voice.
Fill me with Your wisdom and empower
me to fulfill God's will for my life.
Amen.

REFLECTION
How blessed are you this week?

_____
_____
_____
_____
_____
_____
_____
_____
_____
_____
_____
_____

TODO IS :   /   /

WHAT IS MY VIBE LIKE ?
COLOUR IN HOW VIBE YOU ARE FEELING

LOW VIBE   HIGH VIBE

WEEK 34

GOD'S PEACE IN TROUBLE

John 16:33
"I have told you these things, so that in me you may have peace. In this world you will have trouble. But take heart! I have overcome the world."

DEVOTIONAL

In the midst of trials, Jesus offers us peace.
The world may bring challenges and difficulties,
but we can have peace knowing that He has overcome
the world. Our troubles are temporary,
but His peace is eternal. Let your heart be comforted
by His promise, and rest in the assurance
that He is with you, no matter the storm.

PRAYER

Lord,

*Thank You for the peace You offer
in the midst of trouble.
Help me to take heart, knowing that You have
overcome the world.
Calm my fears and let Your peace fill my heart.
Amen.*

REFLECTION

When do you feel connected to the most high?

___
___
___
___
___
___
___
___
___
___
___
___
___
___

TODAY IS :   /   /

WHAT IS MY VIBE LIKE ?
COLOUR IN HOW VIBE YOU ARE FEELING

LOW VIBE   HIGH VIBE

WEEK 35
WALKING IN OBEDIENCE

John 14:15
"If you love me, keep my commands."

DEVOTIONAL

Obedience to God is a sign of our love for Him.
When we follow His commands, we demonstrate our trust
in His wisdom and goodness. Obedience isn't always easy,
but it leads to blessings and growth. As we surrender our
will to God's, we align ourselves with His purpose.
Love Him by walking in obedience, knowing
that His commands lead to life.

PRAYER
Lord,

Help me to love You through obedience.
Give me the strength to follow
Your commands and trust in Your wisdom.
Let my life reflect my love for You.
Amen.

REFLECTION

What are the things you're worried about?

_____
_____
_____
_____
_____
_____
_____
_____
_____
_____
_____
_____

TODAY IS :   /   /

WHAT IS MY VIBE LIKE ?
COLOUR IN HOW VIBE YOU ARE FEELING

LOW VIBE   HIGH VIBE

WEEK 36
THE JOY OF THE LORD

Nehemiah 8:10
"Do not grieve, for the joy of the Lord is your strength."

DEVOTIONAL

The joy of the Lord is not based on circumstances,
but on His presence. In times of sadness,
His joy is our strength. It is a deep, abiding joy that comes
from knowing that we are loved, redeemed, and secure
in Him. When we experience God's joy, it empowers
us to face life's difficulties with hope and perseverance.

PRAYER
Lord,

Fill me with Your joy.
Let it be my strength in times of struggle
and my celebration in times of victory.
May Your joy sustain me as I walk through life.
Amen.

REFLECTION

How would you say your friends feels about you?

TODAY IS :   /   /

WHAT IS MY VIBE LIKE ?
COLOUR IN HOW VIBE YOU ARE FEELING

LOW VIBE　　　　　　　　　　　　　　　　　HIGH VIBE

WEEK 37
GOD'S ETERNAL LOVE

Romans 8:38-39
"For I am convinced that neither death nor life, neither angels nor demons, neither the present nor the future, nor any powers, neither height nor depth, nor anything else in all creation, will be able to separate us from the love of God that is in Christ Jesus our Lord."

DEVOTIONAL

God's love is eternal and unshakeable.
Nothing in this world can separate us from His love.
In times of uncertainty, we can hold fast to the truth that
His love remains constant, unwavering, and
all-encompassing. No matter what we face,
His love will carry us through.
Let this truth anchor your heart and give you peace.

PRAYER
Lord,

Thank You for Your eternal love. I am so grateful that nothing can separate me from You. Help me to rest in Your love and find peace in Your unchanging affection. Amen.

REFLECTION

Do you notice even the smallest inconsistencies and errors in my work and how do you fix it?

_____
_____
_____
_____
_____
_____
_____
_____
_____
_____
_____
_____
_____

TODAY IS :   /   /

WHAT IS MY VIBE LIKE ?
COLOUR IN HOW VIBE YOU ARE FEELING

LOW VIBE [ ] HIGH VIBE

WEEK 38
THE COMFORT OF GOD

2 Corinthians 1:3-4
"Praise be to the God and Father of our Lord Jesus Christ, the Father of compassion and the God of all comfort, who comforts us in all our troubles, so that we can comfort those in any trouble with the comfort we ourselves receive from God."

DEVOTIONAL

God is the ultimate source of comfort.
When we are hurting or overwhelmed,
He comes alongside us to bring peace and healing.
His compassion is never-ending, and He meets us where
we are. As we receive His comfort,
we are empowered to comfort others who are going
through similar struggles. Let God's comfort fill your
heart, and share it with those in need.

PRAYER

Lord,

*Thank You for Your comforting presence.
In my times of trouble, remind me that You are near, offering peace and healing.
Help me to share Your comfort with others who need it.
Amen.*

REFLECTION

Are you able to maintain high standards even under tight deadlines.

TODAY IS :   /   /

WHAT IS MY VIBE LIKE ?
COLOUR IN HOW VIBE YOU ARE FEELING

LOW VIBE ⸻⸻⸻⸻⸻⸻⸻⸻⸻ HIGH VIBE

WEEK 39
GOD'S FAITHFUL PROVISION

Philippians 4:19
"And my God will meet all your needs according to the riches of his glory in Christ Jesus."

DEVOTIONAL

God is faithful to provide for all our needs.
Whether physical, emotional, or spiritual,
He is the ultimate provider. When we trust Him,
we can rest assured that He will meet every need according
to His abundant riches. God's provision is always perfect,
timely, and more than enough.

PRAYER
Lord,

Thank You for Your faithful provision in my life.
Help me to trust You to meet all of my needs,
knowing that You are more than enough.
May I be content and thankful
for all that You provide.
Amen.

REFLECTION

Describe yourself the best way you can

_____
_____
_____
_____
_____
_____
_____
_____
_____
_____
_____
_____

TODAY IS :   /   /

WHAT IS MY VIBE LIKE ?
COLOUR IN HOW VIBE YOU ARE FEELING

LOW VIBE   HIGH VIBE

WEEK 40

LIVING IN GOD'S PURPOSE

Jeremiah 29:11
"For I know the plans I have for you," declares the Lord,
"plans to prosper you and not to harm you,
plans to give you a hope and a future."

DEVOTIONAL

God has a unique and wonderful plan for each of our lives.
His purpose is not to harm us, but to prosper
us and give us a future full of hope. Trusting in His plan
requires patience and faith, knowing that He is leading
us step by step to the life He has destined for us.

PRAYER

Lord,

Thank You for the purpose You have for my life. Help me to trust in Your plans and to follow Your guidance with faith and obedience. May I live each day according to Your will and purpose. Amen.

REFLECTION

Do you accept yourself for who you are?

TODAY IS :   /   /

WHAT IS MY VIBE LIKE ?
COLOUR IN HOW VIBE YOU ARE FEELING

LOW VIBE   HIGH VIBE

WEEK 41
GOD'S EVERLASTING LOVE

Psalm 136:26
*"Give thanks to the God of heaven.
His love endures forever."*

DEVOTIONAL

God's love is unshakable and eternal. Paul reminds us in Romans 8:38-39 that nothing—not life's trials, spiritual forces, or any power—can separate us from His love in Christ Jesus. This truth brings peace and strength, especially in times of fear or uncertainty.

God's love doesn't depend on our circumstances or actions; it is steadfast and unwavering. When life feels overwhelming, remember that His love is an anchor for your soul. You are deeply loved, always seen, and never alone. Let this truth give you hope and confidence today.

PRAYER

Heavenly Father,

Thank You for Your endless love that nothing can separate me from.
Remind me of Your presence when I feel weak or distant.
Help me trust in Your faithfulness and reflect Your love to others.
In Jesus' name, Amen.

REFLECTION

What are your achievements and are you proud of it?

_____
_____
_____
_____
_____
_____
_____
_____
_____
_____
_____
_____

TODAY IS :   /   /

WHAT IS MY VIBE LIKE ?
COLOUR IN HOW VIBE YOU ARE FEELING

LOW VIBE | | HIGH VIBE

WEEK 42
PURSUING PEACE

Romans 12:18
"If it is possible, as far as it depends on you, live at peace with everyone."

DEVOTIONAL

God calls us to pursue peace in all our relationships. It's not always easy, but we are to do our part in fostering peace. When conflict arises, seek resolution with grace, understanding, and patience. Living at peace with others brings honor to God and reflects His love in our lives.

PRAYER

Lord,

Help me to pursue peace in all my relationships.
When conflict arises, give me wisdom
and grace to resolve it.
May my life reflect Your peace
and love to those around me.
Amen.

REFLECTION

Do you love yourself life?

TODAY IS :   /   /

WHAT IS MY VIBE LIKE ?
COLOUR IN HOW VIBE YOU ARE FEELING

LOW VIBE   HIGH VIBE

WEEK 43
TRUSTING GOD'S PLANS

Jeremiah 29:11
"For I know the plans I have for you," declares the Lord,
"plans to prosper you and not to harm you,
plans to give you a hope and a future."

DEVOTIONAL

God's plans for our lives are always good,
even when we can't see the full picture.
Trust that He has a purpose for every season of your life,
and that His plans will lead to your growth and fulfillment.
When you feel uncertain, hold on to His promise that
He has good things in store for you.

PRAYER
Lord,

*Thank You for Your plans for my life.
Help me to trust in Your guidance,
even when I don't understand.
I believe You are leading me to a hope-filled future.
Amen.*

REFLECTION

Are you satisfied with your body?

TODAY IS :   /   /

WHAT IS MY VIBE LIKE ?
COLOUR IN HOW VIBE YOU ARE FEELING

LOW VIBE ⬜ HIGH VIBE

WEEK 44
ABIDING IN CHRIST

John 15:5
"I am the vine; you are the branches.
If you remain in me and I in you, you will bear much fruit;
apart from me you can do nothing."

DEVOTIONAL

Abiding in Christ is the key to spiritual growth and fruitfulness. When we remain connected to Him, we draw strength, wisdom, and love.
Without Him, we can do nothing.
The more we abide in Him, the more we reflect His love and character in our lives.

PRAYER
Lord,

Help me to remain in You.
Strengthen my connection with You so that
I may bear much fruit for Your kingdom.
Teach me to abide in Your presence daily.
Amen.

REFLECTION

Do you have self-awareness or is it something you're working towards?

TODAY IS :   /   /

WHAT IS MY VIBE LIKE ?
COLOUR IN HOW VIBE YOU ARE FEELING

LOW VIBE ⎯⎯⎯⎯⎯⎯⎯⎯⎯⎯⎯⎯⎯⎯⎯⎯⎯⎯⎯⎯⎯⎯ HIGH VIBE

WEEK 45
NEW BEGINNINGS

Isaiah 43:19
"See, I am doing a new thing! Now it springs up;
do you not perceive it?"

DEVOTIONAL

God is always doing something new in our lives.
He is constantly working to bring about new opportunities,
growth, and blessings. Embrace the new beginnings
He is bringing into your life. Be open to His leading
and trust that His plans are always for your good.

PRAYER
Lord,

*Thank You for the new beginnings
You bring into my life.
Help me to embrace the changes You are making
and trust in Your direction.
I believe You are doing a new thing in me.
Amen.*

REFLECTION

Do you ask for help when you need it?

_____
_____
_____
_____
_____
_____
_____
_____
_____
_____
_____
_____

TODAY IS :   /   /

WHAT IS MY VIBE LIKE ?
COLOUR IN HOW VIBE YOU ARE FEELING

LOW VIBE   HIGH VIBE

WEEK 46
SHARING GOD'S LOVE

1 John 4:7-8
*"Dear friends, let us love one another,
for love comes from God. Everyone who loves has been
born of God and knows God. Whoever does
not love does not know God, because God is love."*

DEVOTIONAL

God's love is the foundation of our faith.
As we experience His love, we are called to share
it with others. Love is not just a feeling;
it's an action that reflects God's character.
Let God's love flow through you to those around you,
showing the world His goodness and grace.

PRAYER
Lord,

*Thank You for Your unconditional love.
Help me to share Your love with others,
reflecting Your character in all I do.
May Your love be evident in my life.
Amen.*

REFLECTION
Are you able to express your self freely with your friends?

TODAY IS :   /   /

WHAT IS MY VIBE LIKE ?
COLOUR IN HOW VIBE YOU ARE FEELING

LOW VIBE ☐ HIGH VIBE

WEEK 47
FAITH IN THE STORM

Matthew 14:31
"Immediately Jesus reached out his hand and caught him. 'You of little faith,' he said, 'why did you doubt?'"

DEVOTIONAL

In the storms of life, it's easy to become fearful
and lose faith. But just as Jesus reached out to
Peter when he began to sink, He is there to help us in our
moments of doubt. Trust in His presence and power,
knowing that He will not let you go under.
Keep your eyes on Jesus, even in the storm.

PRAYER
Lord,

When the storms of life come, help me to keep my eyes on You. Strengthen my faith and remind me that You are always with me, ready to catch me when I fall. Amen.

REFLECTION

How do you show you care to others?

TODAY IS :   /   /

WHAT IS MY VIBE LIKE ?
COLOUR IN HOW VIBE YOU ARE FEELING

LOW VIBE   HIGH VIBE

WEEK 48
FORGIVENESS

Ephesians 4:32
"Be kind and compassionate to one another,
forgiving each other, just as in Christ God forgave you."

DEVOTIONAL

Forgiveness is not always easy, but it is essential for healing. When we forgive, we release ourselves from bitterness and pain. Just as God has forgiven us, we are called to forgive others. Let go of any grudges and allow God's peace to restore your heart.

PRAYER
Lord,

*Help me to forgive others as You have forgiven me. Remove any bitterness from my heart and fill me with compassion and kindness. Let Your forgiveness flow through me.
Amen.*

REFLECTION
What is something you'll like to do for yourself more often?

TODAY IS :   /   /

WHAT IS MY VIBE LIKE ?
COLOUR IN HOW VIBE YOU ARE FEELING

LOW VIBE   [   ]   HIGH VIBE

WEEK 49

GOD'S GUIDANCE IN DECISION-MAKING

Proverbs 3:5-6
"Trust in the Lord with all your heart and lean not on your own understanding; in all your ways submit to him, and he will make your paths straight."

DEVOTIONAL

God promises to guide us in every decision we face.
When we trust in Him and seek His will,
He will direct our paths. Our understanding is limited,
but God's wisdom is limitless. By submitting to Him,
we can have confidence that He will lead
us in the right direction.

PRAYER
Lord,

Help me to trust You with all my heart and lean on Your wisdom in every decision I make. Guide me with Your perfect understanding and lead me along the right path.
Amen.

REFLECTION
When do you feel most valued by the people are you you?

_____
_____
_____
_____
_____
_____
_____
_____
_____
_____

TODAY IS :   /   /

WHAT IS MY VIBE LIKE ?
COLOUR IN HOW VIBE YOU ARE FEELING

LOW VIBE   HIGH VIBE

WEEK 50
GRATITUDE IN ALL CIRCUMSTANCES

1 Thessalonians 5:18
"Give thanks in all circumstances;
for this is God's will for you in Christ Jesus."

DEVOTIONAL

Gratitude is a powerful expression of trust in God.
No matter what life brings, we are called to give thanks
in all circumstances. This does not mean we thank
God for the hardships themselves, but we acknowledge
His goodness in the midst of them.
Gratitude aligns our hearts with God's will.

PRAYER
Lord,

Help me to give thanks in every circumstance, trusting that You are good no matter what. Teach me to recognize Your blessings even in difficult times.
Amen.

REFLECTION

What advise would you give your younger self?

TODAY IS :   /   /

WHAT IS MY VIBE LIKE ?
COLOUR IN HOW VIBE YOU ARE FEELING

LOW VIBE | | HIGH VIBE

WEEK 51

THE BEAUTY OF GOD'S CREATION

Psalm 19:1
*"The heavens declare the glory of God;
the skies proclaim the work of his hands."*

DEVOTIONAL

God's creation is a testimony of His greatness and glory. From the beauty of the skies to the wonders of the earth, everything points back to Him. Take time to appreciate the natural world around you, recognizing it as a reflection of God's creativity and majesty.

PRAYER

Lord,

Thank You for the beauty of Your creation. Help me to appreciate the world around me and to see Your handiwork in all things. May I always be reminded of Your greatness through nature. Amen.

REFLECTION

list all the things and people you're thankful for this year

TODAY IS :   /   /

WHAT IS MY VIBE LIKE ?
COLOUR IN HOW VIBE YOU ARE FEELING

LOW VIBE   HIGH VIBE

WEEK 52
THE GLORY OF GOD

Psalm 29:2
*"Ascribe to the Lord the glory due his name;
worship the Lord in the splendor of his holiness."*

DEVOTIONAL

God is worthy of all our praise and worship.
His glory is unmatched, and His holiness fills the heavens
and the earth. As we reflect on the journey of this year,
let us give glory to God for His goodness, faithfulness,
and grace. May our lives be a reflection of His splendor.

PRAYER

Lord,

I give You all the glory and honor.
You are holy, worthy, and faithful.
I worship You in awe and wonder.
May my life bring glory to Your name.
Amen.

REFLECTION

Your manifestos for the new year.

_____
_____
_____
_____
_____
_____
_____
_____
_____
_____
_____
_____
_____
_____
_____

Conclusion

As you complete this 52-week devotional,
pause to reflect on all that God has done
in your life over the past year. The Scriptures,
devotions, and prayers you have engaged with
are seeds planted in your heart, designed to bear
fruit in your faith journey. Remember,
this is not the end but a new beginning—a deeper
walk with God that continues beyond these pages.
Carry the lessons and truths with you,
trusting in God's unchanging love and guidance
as you move forward.

Ajay E Salako

www.ingramcontent.com/pod-product-compliance
Lightning Source LLC
Chambersburg PA
CBHW040159100526
44590CB00001B/4